The Top 10
Bookkeeping Mistakes Business Owner Make

by Steph Wynne

The Top 10 Mistakes Business Owners Make

All rights reserved.

No part of this book may be reproduced, or stored in a retrieval system, or transmitted in any form or by any means, electronic, mechanical, photocopying, recording, or otherwise, without express written permission of the publisher.

Copyright © 2024 Steph Wynne All rights reserved
Published by Skinny Books

Cover and interior images by Canva

For more information:
Skinny Books Publishing
PO BOX 34652
Los Angeles, CA 90034

www.skinnybookspublishing.com

ISBN: 9798327332959

Disclaimer

The information provided in this book is for educational and informational purposes only. It is not intended to be, nor should it be considered, legal or financial advice. Readers should consult with their own legal, accounting, and financial advisors before making any business decisions.

The case studies included are fictitious and are not based on real individuals or events. The characters and events portrayed in this book are fictitious people. Any similarity to real persons, living or dead, is coincidental and not intended by the author.

Table of Contents

Introduction:	5
Mistake #1: Not Keeping Personal and Business Finances Separate	6
Mistake #2: Failing to Keep Receipts and Records	9
Mistake #3: Neglecting Regular Bank Reconciliation	14
Mistake #4: Incorrectly Categorizing Expenses	18
Mistake #5: Not Tracking Cash Flow	22
Mistake #6: Delaying Bookkeeping Tasks	26
Mistake #7: Ignoring Overdue Invoices	30
Mistake #8: Not Backing Up Financial Data	34
Mistake #9: Overlooking Tax Deadlines and Requirements	38
Mistake #10: Trying to Do Everything Yourself	42
The Top 10 Bookkeeping Mistakes Summary	46

Introduction:

Running a small business is challenging, and managing finances can often feel overwhelming. Unfortunately, many small business owners make common bookkeeping mistakes that can lead to significant financial issues.

In this guide, we'll cover the top 10 bookkeeping mistakes and provide tips on how to avoid them, ensuring your business remains financially healthy and compliant.

Mistake #1:
Not Keeping Personal and Business Finances Separate

One of the most common and potentially damaging mistakes small business owners make is not keeping their personal and business finances separate.

This error can lead to a host of problems, including:

1. Inaccurate Financial Records: When personal and business expenses are mixed, it becomes challenging to maintain accurate financial records. This can lead to errors in bookkeeping, making it difficult to track the financial health of the business.

2. Tax Complications: Mixing finances can create significant complications during tax season. Personal expenses may be mistakenly deducted as business expenses, leading to potential audits, fines, and penalties from tax authorities.

3. Legal Issues: In the event of a lawsuit, having mixed finances can result in personal assets being at risk. Maintaining a clear separation helps protect personal assets from business liabilities.

4. Cash Flow Confusion: Combining personal and business finances can lead to confusion about the business's cash flow, making it difficult to manage expenses, budget effectively, and ensure the business's financial stability.

Case Study Jalena's Painful Lesson: Jalena was a passionate entrepreneur who started a small bakery called "Jalena's Delights" from her home kitchen. Her cookies and mouth-watering bread quickly gained popularity, and soon, her small business was thriving.

With orders flooding in, Jalena found herself juggling numerous tasks – from baking and marketing to managing finances.

Amidst the chaos, she made a critical mistake: she didn't open a separate bank account for her business.

At first, it seemed harmless. Jalena used her personal credit card for business supplies and deposited sales revenue into her personal account.

She believed it was convenient and saved her the hassle of maintaining multiple accounts. But as her business grew, so did the complexity of her finances.

Tax season arrived, and Jalena faced a nightmare. Her accountant struggled to distinguish between personal and business expenses.

Receipts were a mess, and bank statements showed a mix of grocery bills, rent payments, and bakery expenses.

The confusion led to inaccurate financial reports and a chaotic tax filing process. Then came the audit. The tax authorities flagged inconsistencies in Jalena's deductions, questioning whether her claimed expenses were genuinely business-related.

The stress was overwhelming.

Jalena spent sleepless nights gathering documents and justifying every expense. The audit not only cost her significant money in fines and penalties but also precious time that could have been spent growing her business.

Worse yet, a legal dispute with a vendor arose. Because Jalena's finances were intertwined, her personal savings were now at risk.

The vendor's lawyer argued that her personal assets could be used to settle the business dispute. Jalena felt vulnerable and helpless.

The emotional toll was immense. Jalena's passion for baking turned into a source of anxiety and regret. She feared losing everything she had worked so hard to build.

The joy of running her bakery was overshadowed by the constant worry about financial and legal troubles.

Eventually, Jalena sought help. She hired a professional bookkeeper who guided her through the process of separating her finances.

They set up a dedicated business account, categorized every expense accurately, and implemented a robust bookkeeping system.

Though it was a painful lesson, Jalena regained control over her finances and rebuilt her business on a solid foundation. With of course a large bill from the CPA.

Jalena's story is a grim reminder of the importance of keeping personal and business finances separate. The peace of mind and financial clarity that come from proper bookkeeping are invaluable.

Don't let the convenience of mixed finances jeopardize your business's future. Learn from Jalena's experience and take the necessary steps to protect and grow your business with confidence.

By keeping personal and business finances separate, you can avoid the pitfalls that Jalena experienced. Ensure accurate financial records, simplify tax preparation, protect your personal assets, and maintain clear cash flow management.

Mistake #2:
Failing to Keep Receipts and Records

Although I do tell my clients don't worry about the receipts because they are on their statements. However I would say all items over $500 you should keep receipts.

Now for the nice and clean version or receipts keeping. Failing to keep receipts and proper documentation for business expenses is a prevalent mistake among small business owners.

This oversight can lead to drama and significant issues, including:

1. Difficulty in Substantiating Expenses: Without proper receipts, it becomes challenging to prove that expenses were indeed business-related.

This can result in denied deductions during tax preparation.

2. Inaccurate Financial Records: Receipts provide a detailed account of business transactions. Without them, maintaining accurate financial records becomes problematic, leading to discrepancies and errors in bookkeeping.

3. Tax Audits and Penalties: In the event of a tax audit, having organized receipts and records is crucial.

Inadequate documentation can lead to fines, penalties, and increased scrutiny from tax authorities.

4. Cash Flow Mismanagement: Receipts help track cash outflows. Without them, small business owners may struggle to manage their cash flow effectively, potentially leading to other issues.

5. Inability to Analyze Business Performance: Receipts provide insights into spending patterns. Without them, it becomes difficult to analyze where money is being spent and identify areas for cost-saving.

Case Study Tony's Troubles with Tax Time: Tony was the owner of a small yet successful landscaping business called "Tony's Green Thumb." Known for his fabulous garden designs and reliable service, Tony's business was growing steadily.

However, while hustling projects and meeting new clients, Tony neglected one critical aspect of his business: keeping receipts and records.

Tony believed he could rely on his bank statements and memory to track his expenses. He often discarded receipts or stuffed them into a drawer, thinking he would organize them later.

That "later" never came. Months passed, and Tony's drawer of receipts turned into a chaotic mess.

As tax season approached, Tony's anxiety grew. He realized he needed to provide proof for all the business expenses he planned to deduct.

Without receipts, he struggled to remember the specifics of his purchases.

His financial records were incomplete, and his bank statements lacked the detailed information needed to substantiate his claims.

When he met with his expensive accountant, the situation worsened. The accountant explained that many of his deductions might be disallowed without proper receipts.

Tony faced the grim reality of potentially owing more in taxes than anticipated. His heart sank as he realized the financial strain this could impose on his business.

Then came the worst part: a tax audit. The tax authorities requested detailed documentation for several deductions. Tony spent countless hours sifting through his disorganized drawer, trying to piece together the required information.

The stress was overwhelming, and he felt helpless. The audit resulted in several disallowed deductions due to insufficient documentation, leading to substantial fines and penalties.

Tony's savings took a hit, and he had to cut back on essential business expenses to cover the unexpected tax liabilities.

The financial strain impacted his ability to take on new projects, and his business growth stalled.

Emotionally, Tony was exhausted. The joy he once found in transforming gardens was overshadowed by the constant worry about his financial situation.

He felt frustrated and disappointed in himself for neglecting such a crucial aspect of his business.

Determined to never experience such turmoil again, Tony sought professional help. He hired a bookkeeper who implemented a robust system for organizing and maintaining receipts.

They set up digital tools to scan and store receipts, ensuring they were easily accessible and properly categorized.

With this system in place, Tony regained control over his finances and could confidently prepare for tax season.

Tony's scary story is a serious reminder of the importance of keeping receipts and records.

The stress and financial strain of an audit, coupled with the impact on business growth, highlight the necessity of proper documentation.

Don't let the chaos of disorganized receipts jeopardize your business's future. Learn from Tony's experience and take the steps to ensure your financial records are accurate and complete.

By diligently keeping receipts and maintaining proper records, you can avoid the pitfalls that Tony experienced.

Ensure your expenses are substantiated, simplify tax preparation, manage cash flow effectively, and analyze business performance with confidence.

Mistake #3:

Neglecting Regular Bank Reconciliation

Neglecting regular reconciliation of bank statements with accounting records is a common mistake that can lead to significant financial issues for small businesses.

Reconciliation is the process of ensuring that the transactions recorded in your accounting system match those in your bank statements.

When this is neglected, it can cause several problems:

1. Unnoticed Errors: Errors such as duplicate entries, missing transactions, or incorrect amounts can go unnoticed without regular reconciliation.

These errors can accumulate over time, leading to inaccurate financial statements.

2. Cash Flow Issues: Without regular reconciliation, it becomes challenging to get an accurate picture of your cash flow. This can result in cash shortages, overdraft fees, and an inability to make informed financial decisions.

3. Increased Risk of Fraud: Regular reconciliation helps detect unauthorized transactions or fraudulent activity.

Neglecting this process increases the risk of undetected fraud, which can cause serious financial losses.

4. Inaccurate Financial Reporting: Inaccurate financial records due to unreconciled accounts can lead to misleading financial reports. This affects your ability to assess your business's financial health and make strategic decisions.

5. Tax Compliance Issues: Discrepancies in financial records can cause problems during tax season, leading to potential fines, penalties, and audits from tax authorities.

Case Study: Emily's Reconciliation Nightmare

Emily was a passionate entrepreneur who ran a boutique fashion store called "Emily's Chic Boutique."

Her eye for fashion and dedication to customer service made her store a favorite among local fashion enthusiasts.

However, amidst managing inventory, marketing, and customer relations, Emily neglected one crucial aspect of her business: regular bank reconciliation.

Emily assumed that as long as she kept an eye on her bank balance, everything would be fine. She trusted her bank statements and rarely compared them to her accounting records.

Months went by, and Emily felt confident that her business was thriving. Little did she know, a storm was brewing.

One day, Emily received a call from her bank notifying her of several overdraft fees on her account. Confused and stressed, she checked her bank balance and noticed it was significantly lower than she expected.

She quickly realized that she had been relying on incorrect financial information.

Emily decided to dive into her financial records, only to find a tangled mess. Transactions were missing, some were duplicated, and others had incorrect amounts.

The more she looked, the more discrepancies she found. Emily felt overwhelmed and out of her lane.

Then, the worst happened: a trusted employee had been embezzling funds. Because Emily hadn't been reconciling her accounts, the fraudulent transactions had gone unnoticed for months.

The betrayal stung deeply. She felt a mix of anger, sadness, and regret.

Emily's financial situation worsened as she struggled to pay suppliers and manage her store's expenses. The overdraft fees and missing funds drained her savings.

Her dream of expanding the boutique was now on hold, and she faced the daunting task of rebuilding her finances from scratch.

The emotional toll was heavy. Emily felt like she had failed her business, her employees, and herself. The stress affected her health and her ability to enjoy running her boutique.

She questioned her ability to manage her business effectively.

Determined to never face such a crisis again, Emily sought professional help. She hired a bookkeeper who immediately set up a regular reconciliation process.

Together, they went through months of transactions, correcting errors and identifying the fraudulent activity.

With proper reconciliation in place, Emily regained control over her finances and restored her confidence.

Emily's story is a powerful reminder of the importance of regular reconciliation. The financial and emotional strain of neglecting this crucial task can be devastating. Don't let reconciliation errors and fraud jeopardize your business.

Learn from Emily's experience and prioritize regular reconciliation to ensure your financial records are accurate and secure as this is the true key to staying on top of your books.

By committing to regular reconciliation of your bank statements and accounting records, you can avoid the pitfalls that Emily experienced.

Ensure accurate financial records, detect errors and fraud early, maintain healthy cash flow, and comply with tax regulations.

Mistake #4:
Incorrectly Categorizing Expenses

Incorrectly categorizing expenses is a prevalent mistake that can have significant repercussions for small businesses:

1. Misleading Financial Statements: Proper expense categorization is essential for accurate financial reporting. Misclassified expenses can distort financial statements, making it difficult to assess the true financial health of the business.

This can lead to poor decision-making and missed opportunities for growth and improvement.

2. Tax Problems: Tax filings depend heavily on accurate expense categorization. Misclassifications can result in incorrect deductions, which can trigger audits, penalties, and fines from tax authorities.

You might miss out on eligible deductions or incorrectly claim ineligible ones, which can increase your tax liability and cause financial strain.

3. Poor Financial Analysis: Understanding where your money is going is crucial for effective financial management. Incorrectly categorized expenses can obscure spending patterns, making it difficult to identify areas where you can cut costs or invest more.

This can lead to inefficient use of resources and hinder the growth of your business.

4. Cash Flow Issues: Accurate expense categorization helps in better cash flow management. When expenses are miscategorized, it can be challenging to track and manage cash outflows effectively, leading to potential cash shortages and financial instability.

Case Study Markus's Misclassified Madness: Markus was the passionate owner of "Tech Innovators," a small but rapidly growing tech startup known for its innovative software solutions.

His technical expertise was unmatched, but when it came to managing the financial aspects of his business, Markus often felt out of his depth.

Markus believed he could handle the bookkeeping tasks on his own. He used a basic spreadsheet to track his expenses and often guessed how to categorize them. He thought it was a minor detail that didn't require much attention.

As long as he recorded the expenses, everything would be fine—at least, that's what he thought.

Months passed, and Tech Innovators continued to grow. Markus was focused on securing new clients and expanding his product line. However, his haphazard approach to categorizing expenses was slowly creating a financial time bomb.

Tax season arrived, and Markus confidently submitted his tax returns, unaware of the storm brewing. A few weeks later, he received a dreaded letter from the tax authorities: he was being audited. The audit revealed that many of his expenses were misclassified.

Marketing costs were lumped together with office supplies, and personal expenses were mixed in with business expenses.

The tax authorities disallowed several deductions, resulting in a hefty tax bill. The penalties and interest piled up, putting a significant strain on Tech Innovators' finances. Mark felt overwhelmed and helpless.

He had to dip into his personal savings to cover the unexpected costs, and the financial hit jeopardized the company's growth plans.

But the financial damage wasn't the only consequence. The audit process was time-consuming and stressful. Markus spent countless hours gathering documents, answering queries, and rectifying mistakes.

His focus shifted from growing his business to surviving the audit. The stress affected his health and his ability to lead his team effectively. The experience left Markus feeling defeated.

His dream of building a successful tech startup was overshadowed by financial woes and stress. He regretted not seeking professional help sooner and realized that his approach to bookkeeping was flawed.

Determined to never face such a crisis again, Markus sought the help of a professional bookkeeper. The bookkeeper meticulously reviewed his financial records, corrected the misclassifications, and implemented a robust system for accurate expense categorization.

With professional guidance, Markus regained control over his finances and could focus on his passion for innovation.

Markus's story is a stark reminder of the importance of correctly categorizing expenses. The financial and emotional toll of misclassified expenses can be devastating.

Don't let poor bookkeeping practices jeopardize your business's future. Learn from Markus's experience and ensure your expenses are accurately categorized to maintain financial stability and support business growth.

By correctly categorizing expenses, you can avoid the pitfalls that Markus experienced. Ensure accurate financial statements, optimize your tax filings, improve financial analysis, and maintain healthy cash flow.

Mistake #5:
Not Tracking Cash Flow

Not tracking cash flow is a critical mistake that can have severe consequences for small businesses. Cash flow refers to the movement of money into and out of your business, and it's crucial for maintaining financial stability and planning for growth.

Here's why tracking cash flow is essential and the problems that arise when it's neglected:

1. Cash Shortages: Without tracking cash flow, businesses can easily run into cash shortages, making it difficult to pay bills, salaries, and other expenses on time. This can lead to late fees, damaged supplier relationships, and operational disruptions.

2. Inability to Make Informed Decisions: Accurate cash flow tracking provides insights into when and how money is entering and leaving the business. Without this information, it's challenging to make informed decisions about spending, investing, and saving.

3. Increased Risk of Insolvency: Poor cash flow management is one of the leading causes of business failure. If cash outflows consistently exceed inflows, the business may face insolvency, where it cannot meet its financial obligations.

4. Missed Opportunities: Not knowing your cash position can cause you to miss out on investment opportunities, bulk purchasing discounts, or new projects that require upfront capital.

Good cash flow management enables you to seize opportunities as they arise.

5. Stress and Uncertainty: Without a clear understanding of cash flow, business owners often experience high levels of stress and uncertainty. The constant worry about whether there will be enough cash to cover expenses can take a toll on your health and well-being.

Case Study Lisa's Cash Flow Crisis: Lisa was the proud owner of "Lisa's Sweet Treats," a bakery known for its delectable proprietary candy and cakes.

Her talent for baking was unmatched, and her business quickly gained a loyal customer base.

Despite her success, Lisa had one major blind spot: she didn't track her cash flow. Lisa assumed that as long as her sales were strong, her business would be fine.

She focused on creating new recipes and expanding her menu, confident that the profits would follow. She kept an eye on her bank balance but never took the time to understand the flow of money in and out of her business.

One month, Lisa decided to take on a large order for a corporate event. She was excited about the opportunity and invested heavily in premium ingredients and additional staff to fulfill the order.

However, she didn't account for the delay between incurring these expenses and receiving payment from the client.

As the end of the month approached, Lisa found herself in a cash crunch. Bills started piling up—rent, utilities, supplier invoices, and payroll.

She realized too late that she didn't have enough cash on hand to cover these expenses. The corporate client's payment was delayed, leaving her without the funds she desperately needed.

Lisa's stress levels skyrocketed.

She had to scramble to find ways to keep the business afloat. She maxed out her personal credit cards and took out a high-interest short-term loan, hoping it would be enough to bridge the gap.

The financial strain affected her ability to focus on her baking, and the quality of her products began to suffer. The loan and credit card debt quickly accumulated interest, further exacerbating her cash flow problems.

Lisa found herself trapped in a vicious cycle of debt. Her dream of running a successful bakery turned into a nightmare. She felt helpless, constantly worried about how she would pay her bills and keep her business running. The emotional toll was immense.

Lisa's passion for baking was overshadowed by the stress of financial uncertainty. She lost sleep, her health declined, and her once-thriving bakery began to lose customers due to declining product quality.

Desperate for a solution, Lisa sought the help of a professional bookkeeper. The bookkeeper introduced her to cash flow tracking and management tools.

They created a cash flow forecast, identifying periods of cash shortages and surpluses. With a clear understanding of her cash flow, Lisa could plan her expenses more effectively and avoid future crises.

Lisa's story is a powerful reminder of the importance of tracking cash flow. The financial and emotional strain of not knowing your cash position can be devastating. Don't let poor cash flow management jeopardize your business.

Learn from Lisa's experience and implement a robust cash flow tracking system to ensure your business's financial stability and growth.

By diligently tracking your cash flow, you can avoid the pitfalls that Lisa experienced. Ensure you have enough cash on hand to cover expenses, make informed financial decisions, and seize growth opportunities.

Mistake #6:
Delaying Bookkeeping Tasks

Delaying bookkeeping tasks is a common mistake among small business owners that can lead to significant problems:

1. Inaccurate Financial Records: When bookkeeping tasks are delayed, financial records become incomplete and inaccurate. This makes it challenging to understand the business's financial health and make informed decisions.

2. Increased Stress and Overwhelm: Procrastinating on bookkeeping tasks leads to a backlog, causing stress and overwhelm. The larger the backlog, the more daunting it becomes to catch up.

3. Missed Deadlines and Penalties: Delayed bookkeeping can result in missed tax filing deadlines and other financial reporting requirements, leading to penalties, fines, and interest charges.

4. Poor Cash Flow Management: Without timely bookkeeping, it becomes difficult to track cash flow accurately. This can result in cash shortages and an inability to meet financial obligations.

5. Inability to Secure Financing: Accurate and up-to-date financial records are crucial for securing loans or attracting investors. Delayed bookkeeping can hinder access to much-needed financing for business growth.

Case Study Ramon's Bookkeeping Backlog: Ramon was a dedicated and skilled plumber who ran his own business, "Ramon's Reliable Plumbing."

Known for his excellent workmanship and customer service, Ramon had built a solid reputation and a steady stream of clients.

However, amidst the demands of running his business and attending to plumbing emergencies, Ramon often neglected his bookkeeping tasks.

Ramon believed that as long as he was generating income and his bank balance looked healthy, everything would be fine. He thought he could always catch up on the bookkeeping later.

However, later never came. He continued to push his bookkeeping tasks to the bottom of his to-do list, focusing instead on growing his business and serving his customers.

Months passed, and the pile of unrecorded receipts, invoices, and financial documents grew larger. Tax season arrived, and Ramon faced a daunting task. His accountant needed accurate financial records to prepare his tax return, but Ramon's books were a mess.

The stress of catching up on months of bookkeeping was overwhelming. Ramon spent countless late nights sifting through piles of paperwork, trying to make sense of it all.

To make matters worse, Ramon missed the tax filing deadline. He incurred penalties and interest charges, further straining his finances. The financial burden and stress took a toll on his health and his ability to focus on his work.

Ramon's clients began to notice a decline in his responsiveness and quality of service. But the worst was yet to come.

Without accurate financial records, Ramon struggled to manage his cash flow.

He faced cash shortages and had to delay payments to suppliers and employees. The financial instability caused him to lose valuable clients and damaged his reputation.

Ramon's dream of expanding his plumbing business seemed further out of reach. He felt frustrated, overwhelmed, and helpless. The joy he once found in his work was overshadowed by the constant worry about his finances.

Desperate for a solution, Ramon sought the help of a professional bookkeeper. The bookkeeper immediately took over the backlog of bookkeeping tasks, organizing and updating Ramon's financial records.

They implemented a system for regular bookkeeping, ensuring that Ramon's books were always up-to-date.

With the bookkeeper's help, Ramon was able to catch up on his bookkeeping and avoid future backlogs.
He regained control over his finances and could focus on growing his business. The stress and overwhelm began to lift, and

Ramon's passion for his work returned.

Ramon's story is a powerful reminder of the importance of staying on top of bookkeeping tasks.

The financial and emotional strain of delaying bookkeeping can be devastating. Don't let procrastination jeopardize your business's future.

Learn from Ramon's experience and ensure your bookkeeping tasks are done regularly to maintain accurate financial records and support business growth.

By committing to regular bookkeeping, you can avoid the pitfalls that Ramon experienced. Ensure accurate financial records, reduce stress, meet financial deadlines, and maintain healthy cash flow.

Mistake #7:

Ignoring Overdue Invoices

Ignoring accounts receivable is a critical mistake that can severely impact a small business's cash flow and financial stability.

Here are the main issues that arise from neglecting accounts receivable:

1. Delayed Cash Inflows: Ignoring overdue invoices means that money owed to the business remains uncollected for extended periods. This delays cash inflows, which are crucial for covering operating expenses and investments.

2. Increased Bad Debt: Overdue invoices that are not actively pursued can turn into bad debt, meaning the business may never collect the money owed. This directly impacts profitability and financial health.

3. Strained Client Relationships: Failing to follow up on unpaid invoices can lead to misunderstandings and strained relationships with clients. It may also set a precedent that late payments are acceptable.

4. Cash Flow Problems: Without timely collection of accounts receivable, businesses can face cash flow problems, making it difficult to meet financial obligations such as payroll, rent, and supplier payments.

5. Administrative Burden: Letting accounts receivable pile up can create a significant administrative burden when the business finally attempts to collect overdue payments. This can divert resources from more productive activities.

Case Study Ahmad's Accounts Receivable Nightmare: Ahmad was a talented app creator and web designer who ran his own business, "Ahmad's Innovative Solutions." Known for his cutting-edge designs and user-friendly apps, Ahmad quickly gained a diverse clientele.

His business was booming, and he was constantly juggling multiple projects. However, amidst the excitement of new projects and deadlines, Ahmad made a critical mistake: he ignored his accounts receivable.

Ahmad was passionate about his work and trusted that his clients would pay their invoices eventually. He believed that as long as he delivered high-quality work, payments would follow.

So, he focused on creating and designing, pushing the task of following up on unpaid invoices to the back of his mind. Months passed, and Ahmad's list of unpaid invoices grew longer. He started noticing a strain on his cash flow.

Despite having a full roster of clients, he struggled to pay his bills and meet payroll. The stress began to mount as he had to dip into his personal savings to keep the business afloat. Then came the breaking point: a major client who owed Ahmad a substantial amount declared bankruptcy.

The unpaid invoice was now a bad debt, and Ahmad realized he would never see that money. The financial blow was devastating. Ahmad felt betrayed and helpless, knowing that he could have avoided this situation by being more proactive.

The cash flow problems spiraled out of control.

Ahmad couldn't afford to invest in new tools and software, which were essential for maintaining the high standards of his work.

He had to turn down lucrative projects because he lacked the necessary resources. The quality of his work started to decline, and clients began to lose confidence in his ability to deliver on time.

The emotional toll was immense. Ahmad felt overwhelmed by the financial strain and frustrated by his inability to manage his business effectively.

The passion and joy he once found in creating innovative apps and designs were overshadowed by the constant worry about unpaid invoices and cash flow problems. The stress affected his health and his relationships with family and friends.

Determined to turn things around, Ahmad sought the help of a professional bookkeeper. The bookkeeper implemented a robust accounts receivable management system.

They set up automated reminders for overdue invoices, established clear payment terms with clients, and regularly followed up on unpaid invoices.

Ahmad also learned to review his accounts receivable reports regularly, ensuring that he stayed on top of outstanding payments.

With the bookkeeper's help, Ahmad managed to collect most of the overdue payments and avoid future bad debts. His cash flow improved, allowing him to reinvest in his business and take on new projects with confidence.

The administrative burden of chasing unpaid invoices was lifted, and Ahmad could focus on what he loved most: creating and designing innovative solutions for his clients.

Ahmad's story is a powerful reminder of the importance of actively managing accounts receivable.
The financial and emotional strain of ignoring unpaid invoices can be devastating.

Don't let poor accounts receivable management jeopardize your business's future. Learn from Ahmad's experience and implement a system to ensure timely collections and maintain healthy cash flow.

By actively managing your accounts receivable, you can avoid the pitfalls that Ahmad experienced. Ensure timely cash inflows, reduce the risk of bad debt, maintain good client relationships, and avoid cash flow problems.

Mistake #8:
Not Backing Up Financial Data

Not backing up financial data is a critical mistake that can lead to severe consequences for small businesses:

1. Data Loss: Without regular backups, financial data can be lost due to hardware failure, theft, cyber-attacks, or natural disasters. This loss can be catastrophic, resulting in the inability to recover essential financial records.

2. Business Disruption: Losing financial data can disrupt business operations, making it difficult to manage finances, process payroll, and make informed business decisions. This disruption can lead to financial instability and loss of revenue.

3. Compliance Issues: Financial data is often required for tax filings, audits, and other regulatory purposes. Losing this data can result in non-compliance with legal requirements, leading to fines, penalties, and increased scrutiny from authorities.

4. Increased Risk of Fraud: Without proper backups, it can be challenging to detect and investigate fraudulent activities. Regular backups help maintain the integrity of financial records and support internal controls.

5. Customer Trust and Reputation: Losing financial data can damage a business's reputation and erode customer trust. Clients expect their financial information to be handled securely, and data loss can lead to a loss of confidence in the business.

Case Study Darius's Data Disaster: Darius was the charismatic owner of "Darius's Salon," a trendy salon that had become a favorite among locals for its stylish cuts and friendly atmosphere.

Darius had built a thriving business with four skilled contractors who rented chairs in his salon. While Darius was great at running his salon and keeping clients happy, he had a dangerous habit: he drank too much.

Darius often spent his evenings at the local bar, unwinding with a few drinks.

Unfortunately, his drinking habits began to interfere with his ability to manage the business's financial aspects.

One of the critical areas he neglected was backing up his financial data. He kept all his records on a single computer in the salon, believing nothing would ever happen to it.

One fateful night, after a particularly heavy drinking session, Darius forgot to lock up the salon properly. He staggered home, thinking everything would be fine. However, the next morning, he arrived to find the salon broken into.

The thieves had stolen cash, equipment, and the computer containing all his financial records. The realization hit Darius like a ton of bricks.

His entire financial history, client information, payroll records, and tax documents were gone. Panic set in as he tried to comprehend the extent of the loss. Without backups, there was no way to recover the critical data.

The impact was immediate and devastating.

Darius struggled to manage the salon's finances.
He couldn't pay his contractors on time, which led to strained relationships and some of them considering leaving.

He had no records for upcoming appointments, causing confusion

and frustration among clients. The business's reputation began to suffer as word spread about the chaos.

Tax season was around the corner, and Darius had no records to file his taxes. The stress and fear of facing penalties and fines kept him up at night.

The financial strain, combined with his drinking, led to a downward spiral. Darius felt overwhelmed and hopeless, watching his dream of running a successful salon crumble before his eyes.

Determined to salvage his business, Darius sought help from a professional bookkeeper. The bookkeeper helped him reconstruct as much of the financial data as possible and set up a robust system for regular data backups.

They used cloud-based software that automatically backed up all financial records, ensuring that such a disaster would never happen again.

With the bookkeeper's guidance, Darius began to get his business back on track. He also sought help for his drinking problem, recognizing the need to make significant changes in his life.

The experience was a painful wake-up call, but it ultimately led to positive changes in both his personal and professional life.

Darius's story is a powerful reminder of the importance of backing up financial data. The financial and emotional toll of losing critical records can be devastating.

Don't let negligence and poor habits jeopardize your business's future. Learn from Darius's experience and implement a robust data backup system to protect your financial records and ensure business continuity.

By regularly backing up your financial data, you can avoid the catastrophic consequences that Darius experienced. Ensure that your financial records are safe from loss, maintain business continuity, and comply with regulatory requirements.

Mistake #9:
Overlooking Tax Deadlines and Requirements

Overlooking tax deadlines and requirements is a critical mistake that can lead to significant problems for small businesses, including:

1. Penalties and Fines: Missing tax deadlines results in penalties and fines, increasing the financial burden on the business. These penalties can add up quickly and become substantial over time.

2. Increased Risk of Audits: Non-compliance with tax requirements increases the risk of audits and scrutiny from tax authorities. Audits can be time-consuming, stressful, and costly.

3. Cash Flow Issues: Unexpected tax penalties and interest charges can strain cash flow, making it difficult to meet other financial obligations.

4. Legal Issues: Persistent non-compliance can lead to more severe legal issues, including potential litigation and damage to the business's reputation.

5. Stress and Anxiety: The stress and anxiety of dealing with tax issues can affect the business owner's health and ability to manage the business effectively.

Case Study Maria's Tax Compliance Turmoil: Maria was a successful lawyer who owned a boutique law firm, "Maria's Legal Services." Known for her expertise in corporate law, Maria attracted high-end clients and built a reputation for excellence.

She loved luxury and indulged in high-end fashion and accessories, always willing to pay top dollar for the best brands.

However, her busy lifestyle left her little time to manage the financial aspects of her firm.

Trusting her friend over professional credentials, Maria hired her inexperienced friend, Emma, to handle the bookkeeping.

Emma was eager to help and earn some extra money, but she lacked the necessary experience and knowledge to manage the firm's finances effectively.

Maria believed that since Emma was a friend, she would be dedicated and trustworthy.

As the months went by, Emma struggled to keep up with the bookkeeping tasks. She was unaware of the critical tax deadlines and requirements, and she didn't have the skills to manage the firm's complex financial records.

Important tax filings were missed, and no one realized the looming danger.

Tax season arrived, and Maria was confident everything was in order. She continued to focus on her clients and indulged in her love for luxury brands, blissfully unaware of the storm brewing.

One day, she received a letter from the tax authorities: her firm had missed multiple tax deadlines, resulting in significant penalties and fines.

The total amount was staggering, far beyond what Maria had expected.

The financial hit was severe.

The penalties and interest charges put a strain on the firm's cash flow, making it difficult to pay employees and cover other expenses.

Maria had to dip into her personal savings to keep the business afloat. The stress and anxiety were overwhelming. Maria felt betrayed and helpless, regretting her decision to hire an inexperienced friend for such a critical role.

The situation worsened when the tax authorities announced an audit of her firm. The audit process was intrusive and time-consuming.

Maria had to gather financial records, respond to numerous queries, and justify every deduction and expense. The experience was humiliating and exhausting. The stress took a toll on Maria's health and her ability to manage the firm effectively.

Her clients began to notice her distraction and declining performance. Maria's passion for her work was overshadowed by the constant worry about the tax issues. The dream of running a successful law firm was at risk.

Realizing the gravity of the situation, Maria decided to seek professional help. She hired a certified bookkeeper and an experienced tax advisor to manage her firm's finances.

The new team immediately took over, rectifying the past mistakes, and ensuring compliance with all tax requirements. They set up a system for tracking deadlines and preparing timely tax filings.

With professional guidance, Maria's firm regained its financial stability. The penalties and fines were negotiated and reduced, and the audit was successfully resolved.

Maria learned a valuable lesson about the importance of hiring qualified professionals and the risks of overlooking tax deadlines and requirements.

Maria's story is a powerful reminder of the importance of complying with tax deadlines and requirements. The financial and emotional toll of missing tax deadlines can be devastating.

Don't let negligence and poor decisions jeopardize your business's future.

Learn from Maria's experience and ensure your taxes are managed by experienced professionals to maintain financial health and compliance.

By staying on top of tax deadlines and requirements, you can avoid the pitfalls that Maria experienced. Ensure timely tax filings, avoid penalties and audits, maintain healthy cash flow, and focus on growing your business.

Mistake #10:
Trying to Do Everything Yourself

Trying to manage all bookkeeping tasks without professional help is a common mistake among small business owners. This can lead to several problems:

1. Increased Risk of Errors: Without professional expertise, the risk of errors in bookkeeping increases. Mistakes in recording transactions, categorizing expenses, and reconciling accounts can result in inaccurate financial records.

2. Inefficiency: Bookkeeping can be time-consuming, especially for someone who is not trained in it. Attempting to handle all bookkeeping tasks yourself can take away valuable time from core business activities.

3. Stress and Burnout: Juggling multiple responsibilities can lead to stress and burnout. The added pressure of managing finances can affect overall productivity and well-being.

4. Missed Opportunities: Without professional help, small business owners may miss opportunities for tax deductions, financial planning, and growth strategies.

A professional bookkeeper can provide valuable insights and advice.

5. Poor Financial Management: Lack of expertise can lead to poor financial management, resulting in cash flow problems, missed tax deadlines, and difficulty securing financing.

Case Study Oscar's Overwhelming Burden: Oscar was a talented tattoo artist who owned a popular studio called "Ink Boss Tattoos."

Known for his intricate designs and creative flair, Oscar had built a loyal clientele. He loved his work and was passionate about creating art on his clients' skin. However, Oscar made a critical mistake: he didn't take bookkeeping seriously.

Oscar believed that as long as he was bringing in money, everything would be fine. He thought bookkeeping was just a minor task that he could handle on his own.

So, he kept a simple spreadsheet and recorded transactions whenever he had a chance, which was not often. He was more focused on his art and running the studio.

Months went by, and Oscar's bookkeeping tasks piled up. He spent late nights trying to catch up, often making mistakes due to fatigue and lack of expertise.

The stress began to mount, affecting his creativity and performance. He missed tax deadlines, incurring penalties and interest charges. The financial strain started to take a toll on his business.

One day, Oscar received a letter from the tax authorities announcing an audit. Panic set in as he realized his financial records were a mess. He spent countless hours trying to organize receipts, invoices, and bank statements.

The audit process was overwhelming and time-consuming, pulling him away from his clients and studio. The audit revealed several discrepancies and errors in Oscar's financial records. He faced hefty fines and penalties, further straining his finances.

The stress and anxiety were unbearable. Oscar's passion for his work was overshadowed by the constant worry about his financial situation.

The impact on his business was severe. Oscar struggled to pay his bills, suppliers, and employees on time. The quality of his work declined, and he began losing clients. The dream of running a successful tattoo studio was slipping away.

Desperate for a solution, Oscar sought help from a professional bookkeeper. The bookkeeper took over the daunting task of organizing and correcting his financial records.

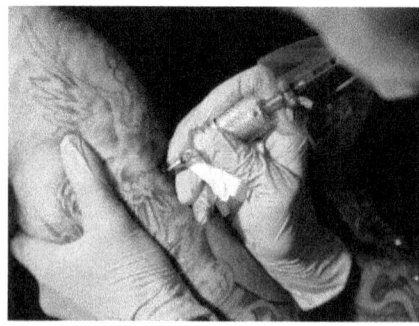

They implemented a proper bookkeeping system, ensuring that all transactions were accurately recorded and categorized. They set up regular financial reporting, helping Oscar stay on top of his finances.

With professional guidance, Oscar's business slowly recovered. He was able to resolve the audit issues, negotiate reduced penalties, and regain control over his finances.

The stress began to lift, and he could focus on what he loved most—creating beautiful tattoos.

Oscar's story is a powerful reminder of the importance of taking bookkeeping seriously and seeking professional help. The financial and emotional toll of trying to manage everything yourself can be devastating.

Don't let poor financial management jeopardize your business's future.

Learn from Oscar's experience and hire a professional bookkeeper to ensure accurate financial records and support business growth.

By recognizing the importance of professional bookkeeping, you can avoid the pitfalls that Oscar experienced. Ensure accurate financial records, reduce stress, avoid penalties, and maintain healthy cash flow.

The Top 10 Bookkeeping Mistakes Summary

1. Not Keeping Personal and Business Finances Separate: Leads to confusion, inaccurate records, and potential tax issues.

2. Failing to Keep Receipts and Records: Results in difficulty substantiating expenses, inaccurate records, and issues during tax time.

3. Neglecting Regular Reconciliation: Causes unnoticed errors, cash flow issues, and increased risk of fraud.

4. Incorrectly Categorizing Expenses: Leads to misleading financial statements, tax problems, and poor financial analysis.

5. Not Tracking Cash Flow: Results in cash shortages, poor decision-making, and increased risk of insolvency.

6. Delaying Bookkeeping Tasks: Leads to inaccurate records, stress, missed deadlines, and poor cash flow management.

7. Ignoring Accounts Receivable: Causes delayed cash inflows, increased bad debt, and cash flow problems.

8. Not Backing Up Financial Data: Results in data loss, business disruption, and compliance issues.

9. Overlooking Tax Deadlines and Requirements: Leads to penalties, fines, increased risk of audits, and cash flow issues.

10. Trying to Do Everything Yourself: Results in errors, inefficiency, stress, missed opportunities, and poor financial management.

Congratulations on making it through "The Top 10 Bookkeeping Mistakes Business Owners Make"!

Congratulations on taking the initiative to improve your bookkeeping practices!

By recognizing and addressing these common mistakes, you're already ahead of the game. Being proactive in your approach will not only help you avoid pitfalls but also position your business for greater success.

Remember, effective bookkeeping is the backbone of a thriving business. Keep learning, stay organized, and don't hesitate to seek help when needed.

Cheers to your success and staying on top of your business finances!

-Steph Wynne

www.ingramcontent.com/pod-product-compliance
Lightning Source LLC
Chambersburg PA
CBHW050246230526
45470CB00005B/2142